What's Inside Yo... Tummy, Mummy?

Abby Cocovini

Contents

This book follows the gestational age of the baby, which is taken from the end of the mummy's last period.

The images in this book only offer a rough guide. Actual size will vary depending on the baby and its mummy.

Introduction

Inside a mummy's tummy is a special place called her womb. A womb is filled with liquid and it's a bit like a warm, squishy cushion.

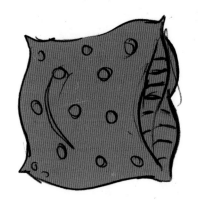

This is where a mummy's baby lives. And it will stay there for nine whole months, growing and changing shape until it is ready to be born.

Turn the pages of this book to find out what happens in the mummy's tummy. And if the mummy holds the book up to her belly, you will see what the baby looks like (actual size) inside her every month!

Just think . . . you used to look like that!

Count the baby's age in days and weeks using the calendar strip at the bottom of each page.

Week Fourteen

| 92 | 93 | 94 | 95 | 96 | 97 | 98 |

9 Months to Go!

That's spring to winter.

Month 1
1-4 weeks

Just a little circle of jelly.

At first the baby is so teeny-tiny, you can't even see it! It doesn't look like a baby yet . . .

It sticks to the side of the mummy's womb and then it starts to **grOW**.

The baby is so small that it has a special name – it's called an embryo.

The baby grows very quickly.
It doubles in size every day for the first four weeks.

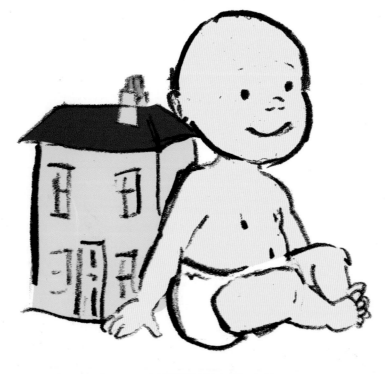

If it did that for nine months, it would be bigger than a house!

The baby is smaller than a grain of rice.

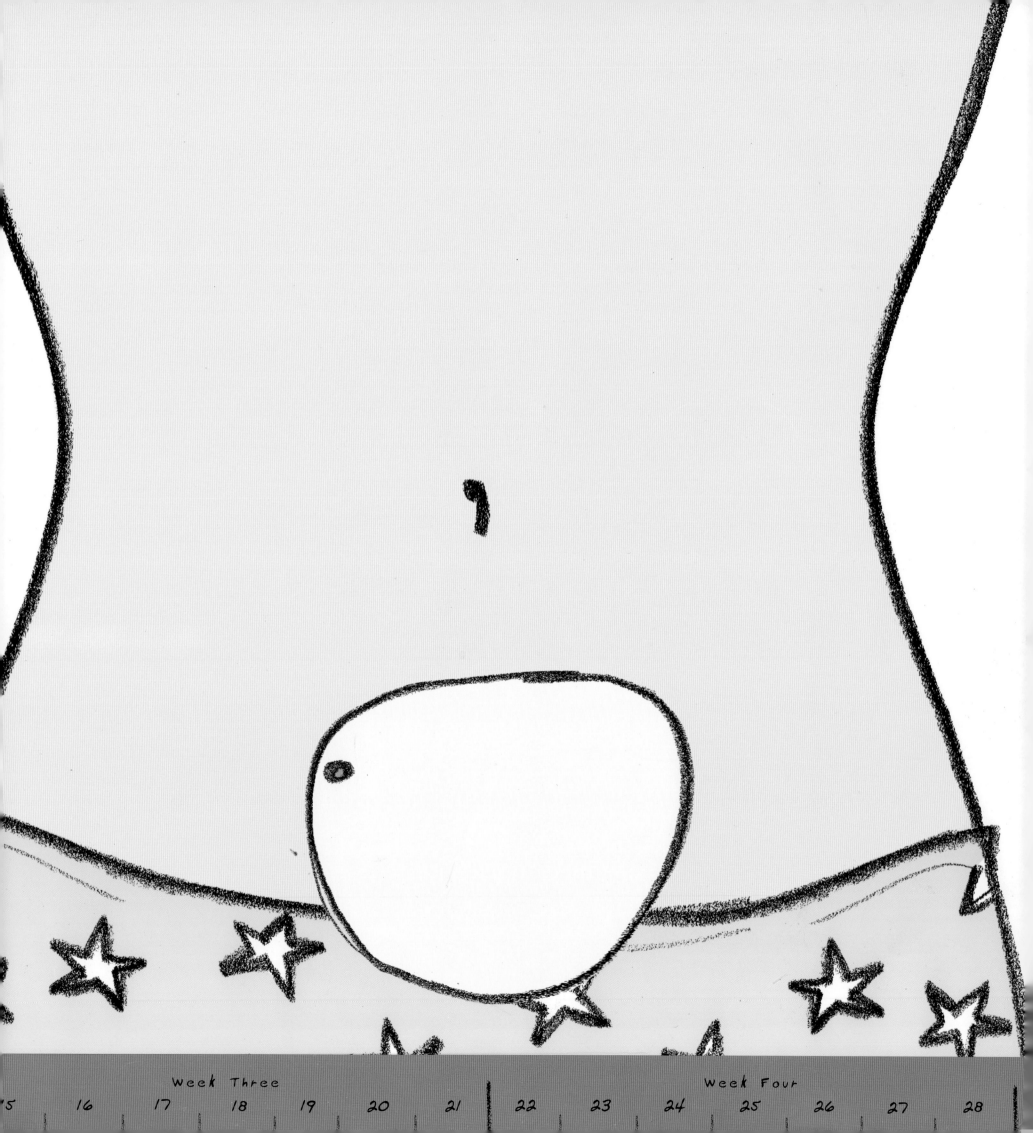

Month 2
5-9 weeks

The baby has grown and changed shape.
It has a big head and a body. But it also has a tail.
It looks a bit like a tadpole!
Don't worry – the tail will go away soon!

It can already turn its head and stretch!

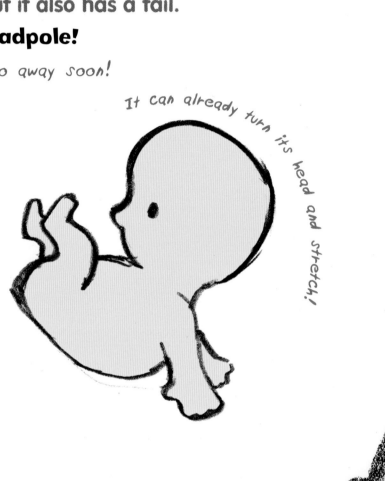

The baby has little bumps on its body,
which are growing into arms and legs.

A tube is growing out of the
baby's belly which sticks to
the side of the womb.

This is the umbilical cord.

It is very important because
it brings food from the
mummy to the baby.

*The baby is
as big as a
baked bean.*

Week Five

Week Six

29 30 31 32 33 34 35 36 37 38 39 40 41 42 43 44 45

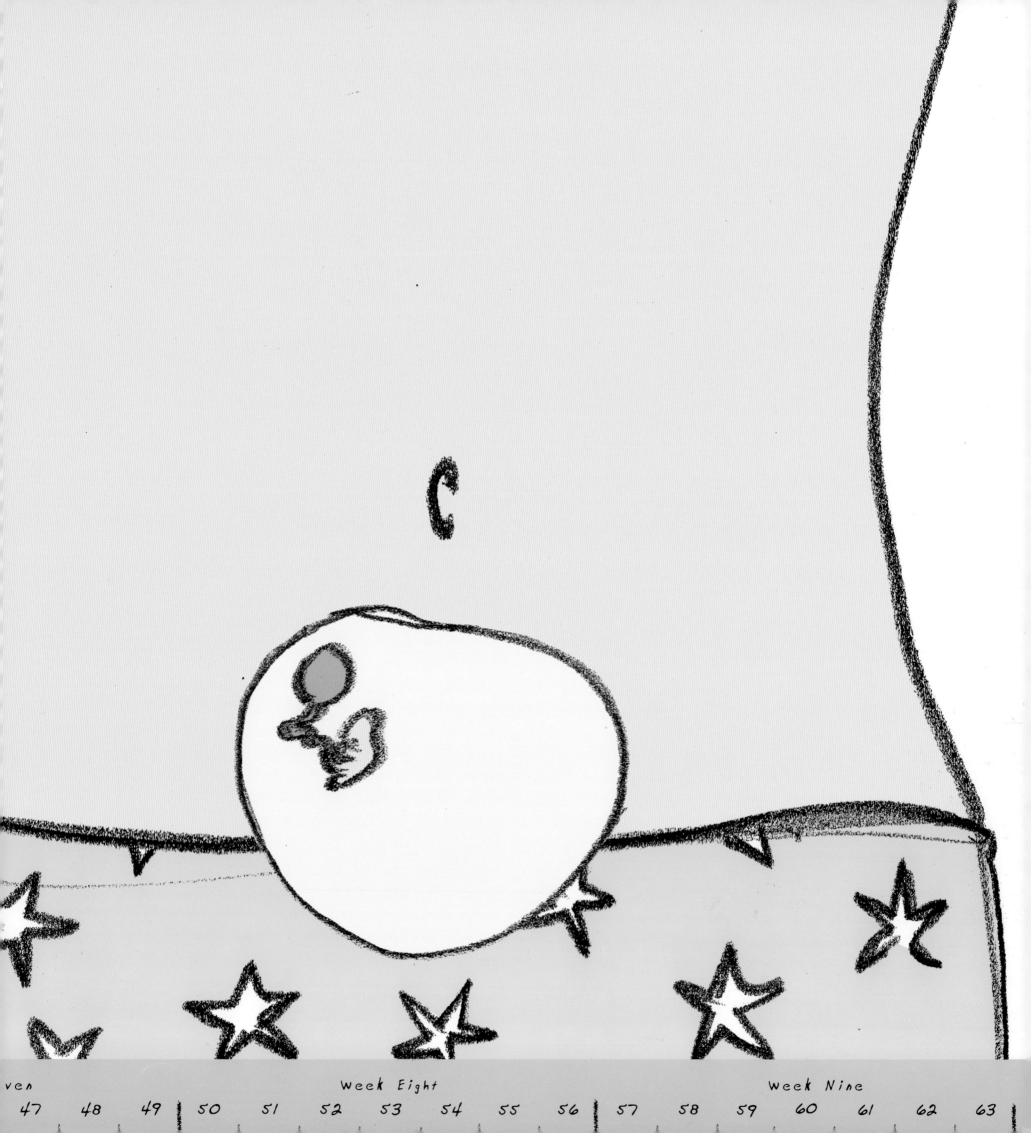

Month 3
10-13 weeks

The baby is as big as an orange.

Now the baby is starting to look more like a baby.

It has lost its tail. It has fingers and toes. It even has fingernails that are as tiny as grains of sand!

There is lots of space in the womb for the baby to move about. It can kick and wriggle around.

But it is still so small, the mummy won't even feel it!

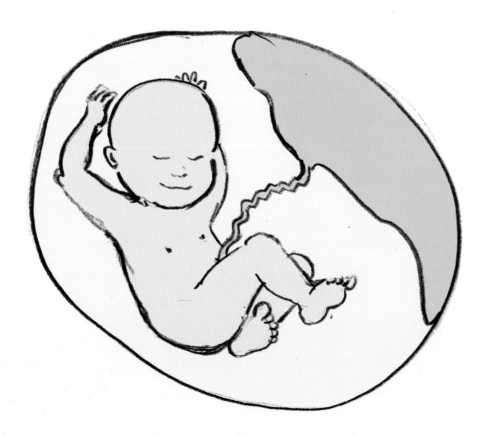

The baby can open and close its mouth and put its hand on its head!

The baby is a bit bigger now. It's as long as a grown-up's finger.

Week Twelve   Week Thirteen

78   79   80   81   82   83   84   85   86   87   88   89   90   91

6 Months to Go!

That's spring + summer.

Month 4

14-18 weeks

The baby is getting fatter and its hair is growing.

The baby does a wee 15 times a day!

Crunch, crunch, crunch

It's starting to hear! But only things from inside its mummy like . . .

her heartbeat thumping . . .

her blood rushing around . . .

da-dum, da-dum, da-dum

or her dinner being swallowed!

It can point its feet, close its hand and even suck its thumb, just like a grown-up baby!

The baby's also good at pulling faces!

The baby is as big as a medium-sized melon.

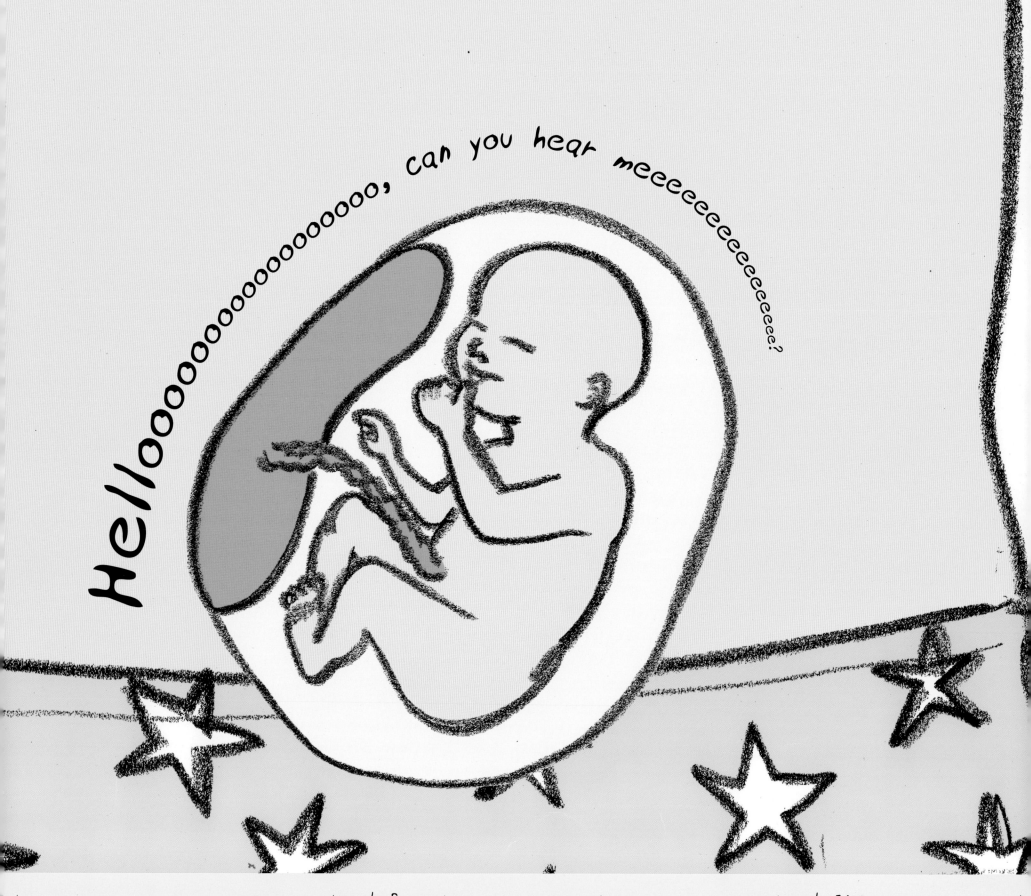

The baby is as big as a 1 litre carton of milk.

Month 5
19-22 weeks

**Now the mummy can feel the baby move!
And if you're lucky, so can you!**

The baby might move when the
mummy rubs her tummy . . .

. . . aaaaaaaaaahhhhhhhhh!

or when the baby hears music . . .

or its mummy's voice . . .

La la la, my special baby

**All sorts of funny things are starting to happen.
Soft, fine hair has grown all over the baby's body.
And now some cheesy stuff covers the
baby's skin to keep it clean.**

But it soon goes - phew!

**The baby
can move its eyes
from side to side.
But it still can't
open them.**

The baby is as big as a large pineapple.

Month 6
23-26 weeks

The baby's getting **bigger!**

And there's not much space to move around. So you might see the baby moving, in the mummy's tummy!

The baby is sleeping a lot.
And it could be dreaming!

It often goes to sleep when its mummy walks about, because the walking rocks it back and forth.

Now the baby can open its eyes!

And it might even turn its head if you shine a light at the mummy's tummy!

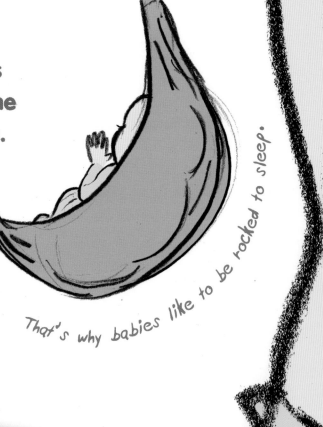

That's why babies like to be rocked to sleep.

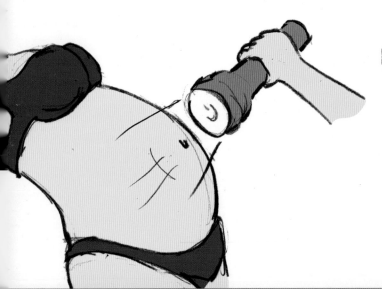

If you put your ear to the mummy's belly, you might hear the baby's heartbeat.

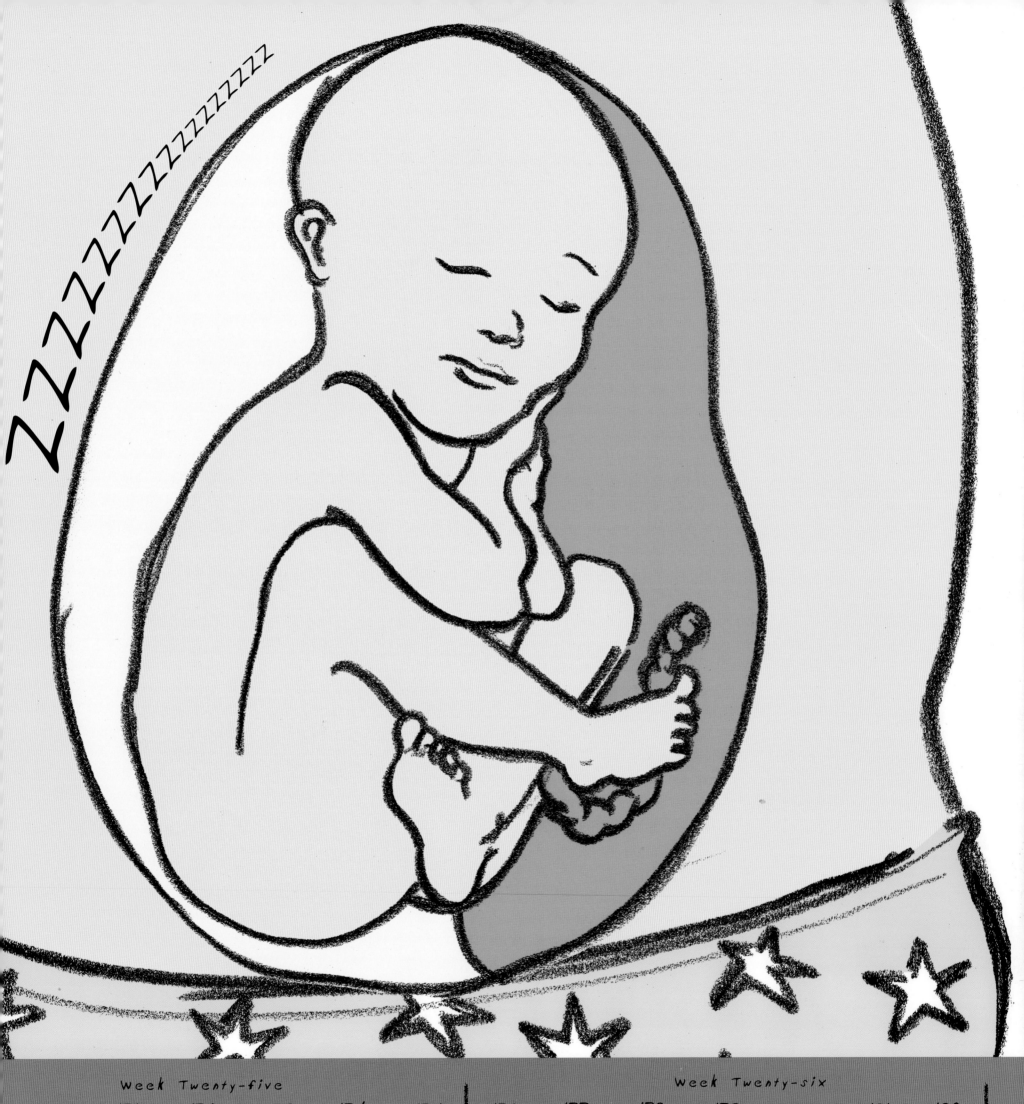

3 Months to Go! That's a whole summer.

Month 7
27-31 weeks

The baby is getting **bigger** and **fatter!**

It can blink its eyes and watch things moving, like a bright light!

It doubles its weight this month. That's like a ten-year-old boy turning into a man in just four weeks!

The baby knows its mummy's voice. And it might remember songs or sounds that it hears a lot.

Twinkle, twinkle, little star...

How I wonder, what you are....

Most of the time the baby just sleeps. It only wakes up for two hours a day.

That's like only waking up for lunch and dinner!

The baby is as big as a loaf of bread.

BREAD

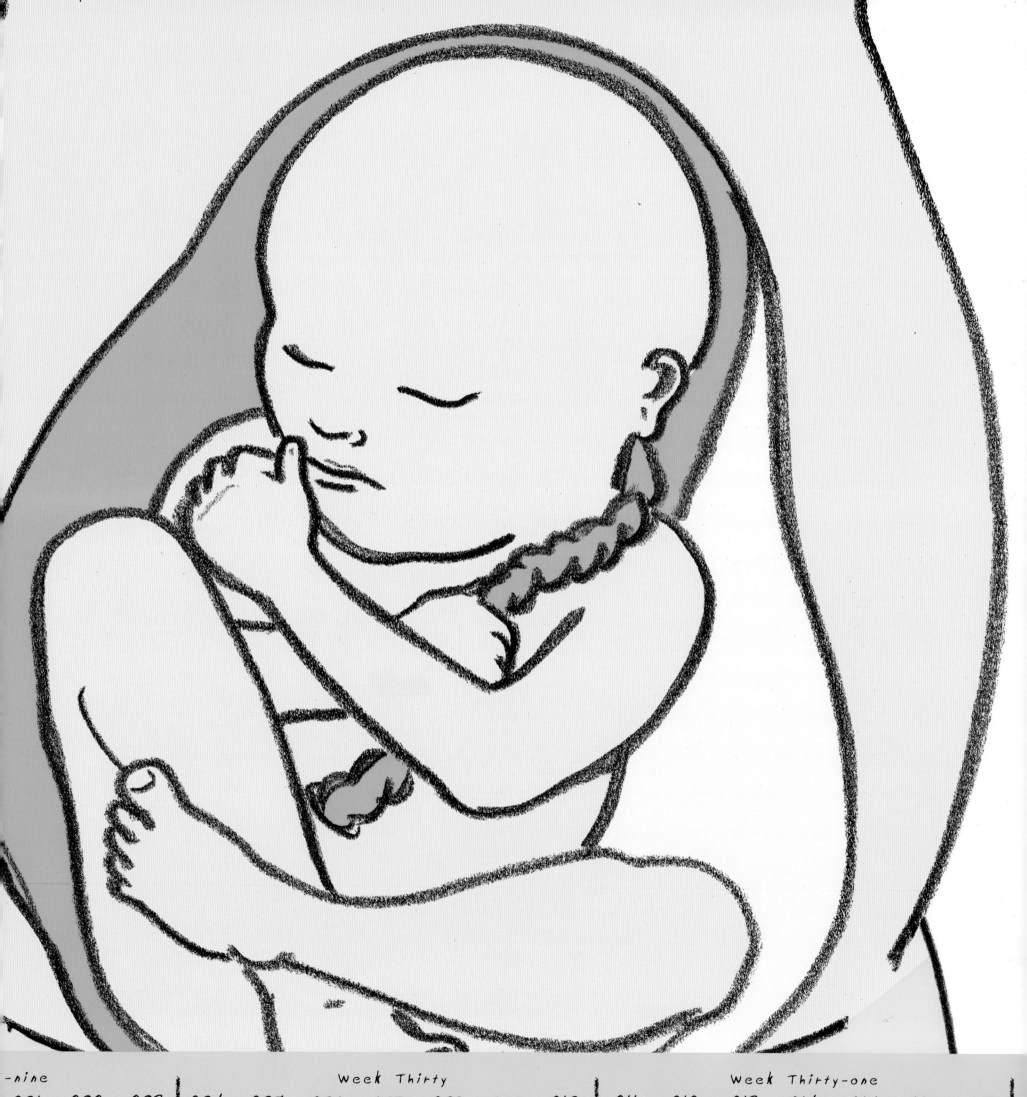

Month 8
32-36 weeks

The baby is **bigger** than ever!

The baby is as big as a pumpkin.

It's starting to see things more clearly, like its hands and fingers.

Its fingernails have grown so long that it can even scratch itself!

The baby has learned so many things . . . listening . . . blinking . . .

The baby stays upside down now so there's more room for its head, and so it is ready to come out of the mummy head first.

And now it's doing all these things as much as it can. Sometimes for nearly half an hour at a time! Phew!

stretching . . .

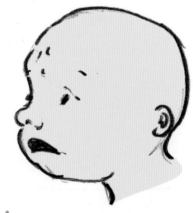

frowning . . .

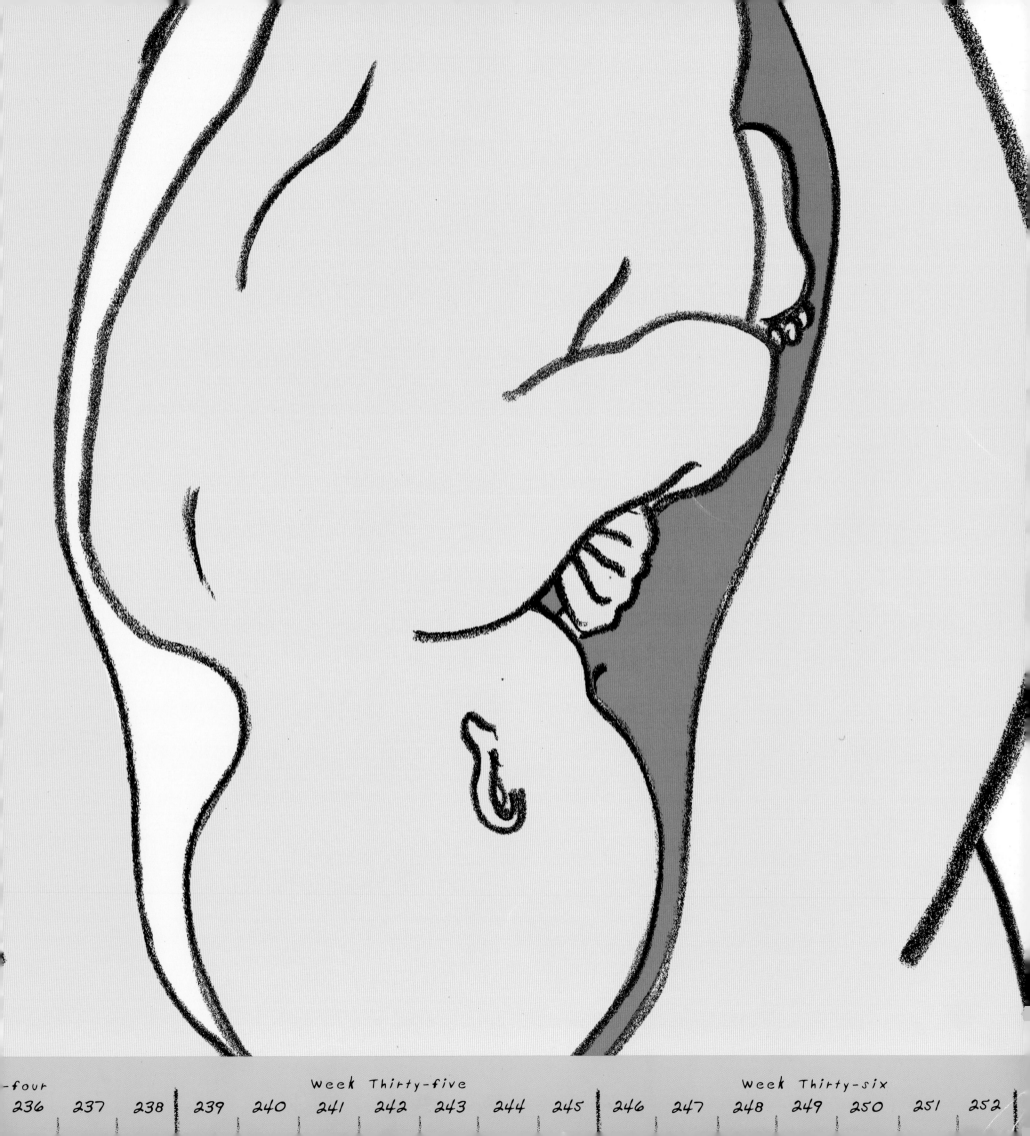

Month 9
37-40 weeks

Now the baby is ready to come out!

It is so big that there is hardly any room to move about.
But it's still looking and listening and blinking and frowning!

The baby is getting ready for its birth day.

The hair and cheesy stuff on the baby's body is falling off. Phew!

When the time is right, the mummy starts to squeeze the baby out.

It's a lot of hard work!

At last the baby comes out of the mummy's tummy!

Hip, hip, **hooray!**

(And about time too)

It's as big as . . .
a baby!

Push!
Push!
Push!

Push!

Push!

It's a Baby!

The newborn baby won't do much except sleep. And don't worry if it cries a lot! Babies can't talk so they cry when they want something instead.

Mostly they want food or their nappy changing.

The baby's first poos are dark green and really sticky! Ew! But after that they're not so bad. Can you help change the baby's nappy?

The baby is hungry all the time! It eats about 9 meals a day. *But it only ever has milk!*

Newborn babies are very small so you have to be very careful with them. You can talk to them, or sing to them, or read them a story. But remember to be quiet when the baby's asleep so you don't wake it up!

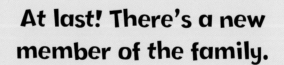

Tra-la-la!

At last! There's a new member of the family.

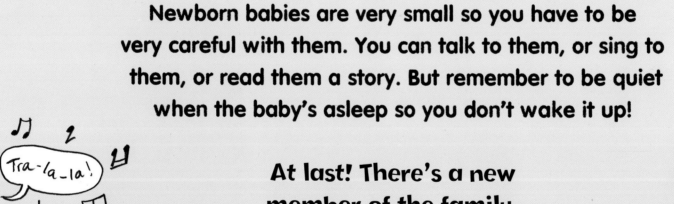

Index and Glossary